THERE IS NO RIGHT WAY TO MEDITATE

YUMI SAKUGAWA

Andrews McMeel
PUBLISHING®

Andrews McMeel Publishing
a division of Andrews McMeel Universal
1130 Walnut Street, Kansas City, Missouri 64106

www.andrewsmcmeel.com

23 24 25 26 27 TEN 10 9 8 7 6 5 4 3 2 1

ISBN: 978-1-5248-7505-3

Library of Congress Control Number: 2022948761

Editor: Katie Gould
Designer: Julie Barnes
Production Editor: Jennifer Straub
Production Manager: Tamara Haus

ATTENTION: SCHOOLS AND BUSINESSES
Andrews McMeel books are available at quantity discounts with
bulk purchase for educational, business, or sales promotional use.
For information, please e-mail the Andrews McMeel Publishing
Special Sales Department: sales@amuniversal.com.

TABLE OF CONTENTS

HI

BENEATH
THE SOUND
OF MY
THOUGHTS

AND

BENEATH
THE SOUND
OF YOUR
THOUGHTS

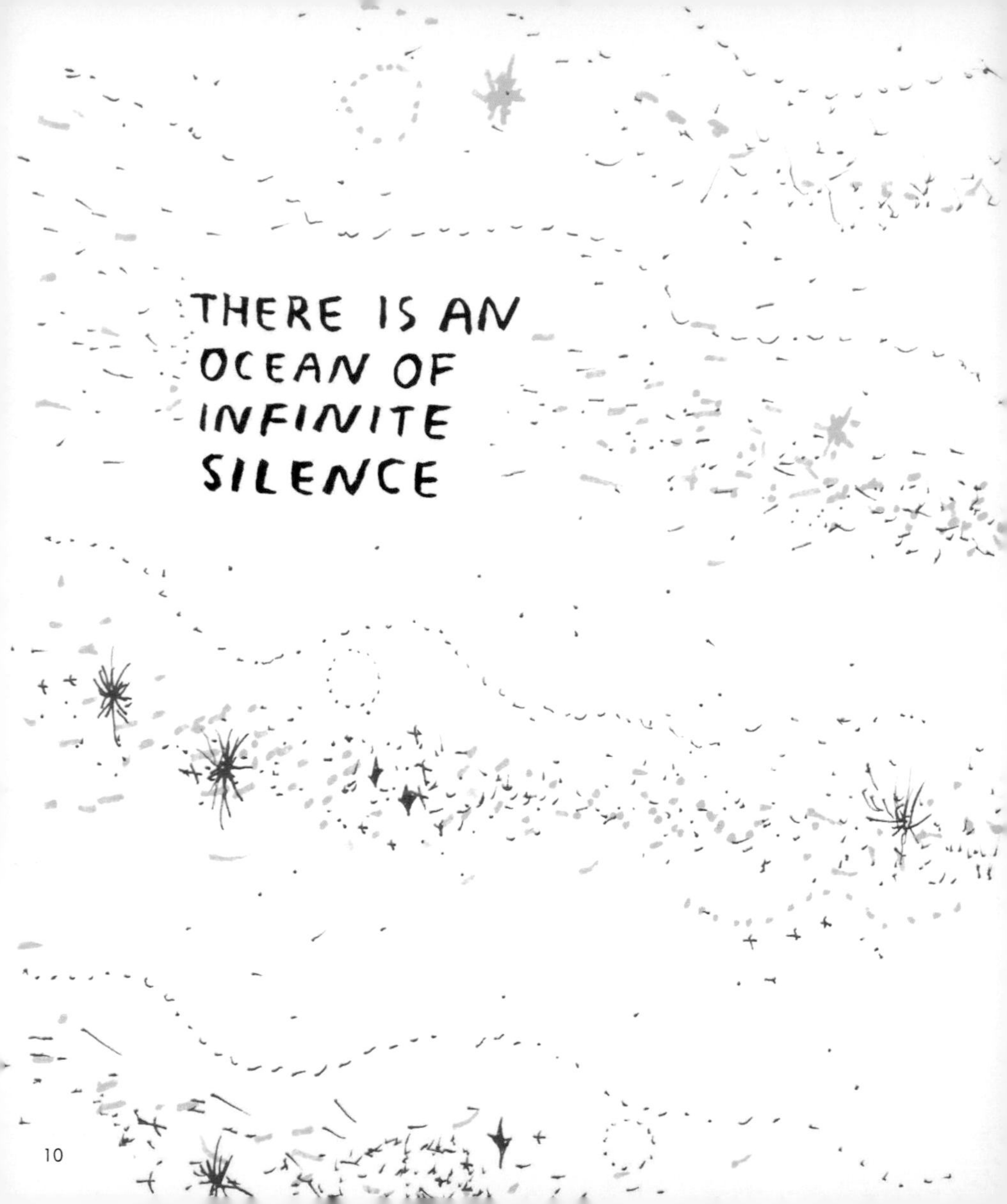

THERE IS AN
OCEAN OF
INFINITE
SILENCE

CONNECTING
US TO EVERYONE
AND EVERYTHING
WE KNOW

AND

EVERYTHING AND
EVERYONE WE
DON'T KNOW

RIGHT THIS MOMENT

CLOSE YOUR EYES

TURN DOWN THE VOLUME OF YOUR INNER THOUGHTS

TURN UP THE VOLUME OF THE INFINITE SILENCE ALL AROUND YOU AND WITHIN YOU

BENEATH THE SOUND OF
OUR OWN THOUGHTS WE
ARE ONE AND THE SAME

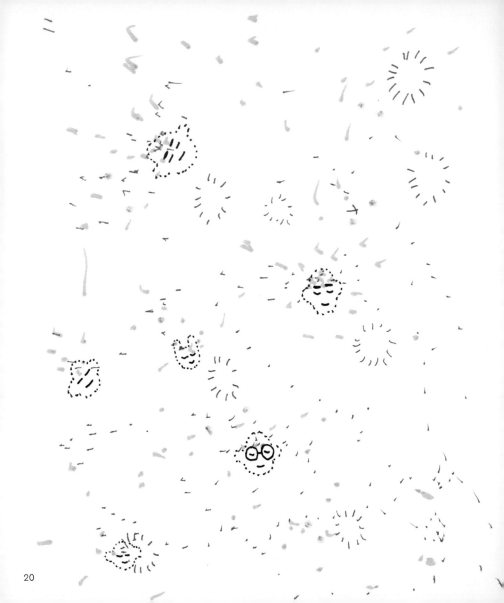

23

INTRODUCTION

BEFORE I TELL YOU HOW TO MEDITATE

(AND HOW THERE IS NO RIGHT WAY TO MEDITATE),

I THOUGHT I WOULD SHARE WITH YOU ALL A LITTLE BIT ABOUT MYSELF AND MY OWN MEDITATION JOURNEY.

HI! I'M YUMI (THE AUTHOR).

I AM A SECOND-GENERATION JAPANESE-OKINAWAN AMERICAN INTERDISCIPLINARY ARTIST LIVING IN LOS ANGELES.

I HAVE BEEN MEDITATING FOR WELL OVER 15 YEARS NOW.

NOWADAYS, I CAN'T IMAGINE GOING THROUGH MY LIFE WITHOUT A DAILY MEDITATION PRACTICE.

SLEEP → WAKE UP → ✧MEDITATE✧

LEARNING MEDITATION HAS BEEN ONE OF THE BEST THINGS I HAVE EVER DONE FOR MY MENTAL HEALTH, CREATIVITY, AND OVERALL SENSE OF HAPPINESS AND WELLBEING.

I DISCOVERED MEDITATION A YEAR AFTER
GRADUATING FROM COLLEGE. I WAS WORKING
ABROAD IN JAPAN AS A CONVERSATIONAL
ENGLISH LANGUAGE TEACHER AND I WAS
DEPRESSED OUT OF MY MIND.

• FAILING
MISERABLY
AT JOB

• FEELING
ISOLATED
AND ALONE

• ART SCHOOL
GRADUATE =
ZERO CLUE
WHAT TO DO WITH
LIFE

• NO REAL
ACCESS TO
SUPPORT SYSTEMS
I HAD IN COLLEGE —
FRIENDS, THERAPY, MEDICATION,
COMMUNITY

you are wrong what is wrong with you you can't do anything right that is why people don't like you there is somet [image: unhappy face] inherently wrong with you and [image: unhappy face] there is so much to fix

I HAD NO IDEA HOW TO TURN OFF THE NEVER-ENDING STREAM OF SELF-LOATHING THOUGHTS THAT TOLD ME EVERY WAKING MOMENT THAT I WAS A WORTHLESS FAILURE.

BLAH BLAH BLAH SELF LOATHING BLAH BLAH BLAH SELF LOATHING BLAH BLAH AH SELF LOATHING BLAH BLAH BLAH SELF LOATHING BLAH BLAH BLAH BLAH BLAH BLAH SELF LOATHING BLAH BLAH BLAH SELF LOATHING BLAH BLAH BLAH SE

what is wrong with me?

IT JUST SO HAPPENED, IN THE MYSTERIOUS WAYS OF THE UNIVERSE, THAT A COLLEAGUE OF MINE LENT ME A COPY OF SPIRITUAL AUTHOR ECKHART TOLLE'S BOOK *A NEW EARTH* WHICH INTRODUCED ME TO A MIND-BLOWING CONCEPT THAT WOULD CHANGE MY LIFE...

YOU ARE NOT YOUR THOUGHTS

YOU ARE THE SPACE BETWEEN YOUR THOUGHTS

WHAT A RELIEF TO KNOW FOR THE FIRST TIME EVER IN MY LIFE THAT MY NEGATIVE THOUGHTS ABOUT MYSELF (OR ANY THOUGHTS, FOR THE MATTER) ARE NOT A 100% ACCURATE REPRESENTATION OF REALITY.

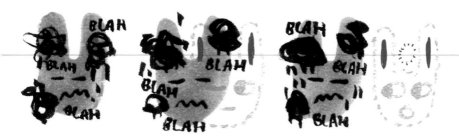

IN REALIZING THAT MY SELF-LOATHING THOUGHTS ARE NOT AN IRON-CLAD REFLECTION OF REALITY SIMPLY BY PAYING EXTRA ATTENTION INWARD, I BECAME CURIOUS ABOUT WHAT OTHER PROFOUND SHIFTS COULD OCCUR IF I PAID MORE ATTENTION AND CONNECTED MORE TO MY INNER SILENCE.

I BEGAN TO EXPERIMENT SITTING
MORE AND MORE IN MY INNER
SILENCE WITH A DAILY MEDITATION
PRACTICE.

THE NEW OPENINGS BREAKING THROUGH
MY DEEPLY ENTRENCHED THOUGHT
PATTERNS PLANTED SEEDS FOR NEW
DESIRES AND NEW THOUGHTS, WHICH
LEAD TO NEW ACTIONS THAT SHIFTED
MY INNER AND OUTER WORLD TO
A MORE SELF-LOVING STATE OF MIND.

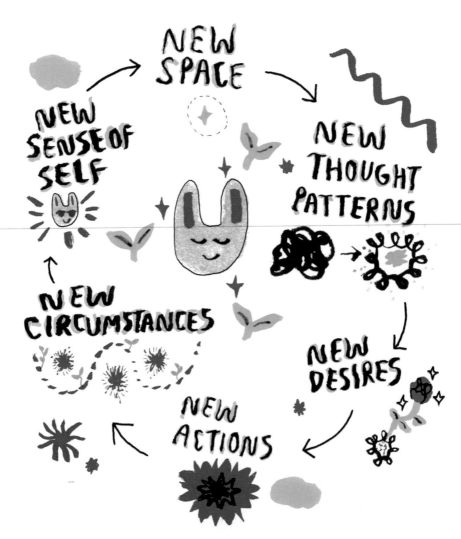

NEW SPACE

NEW SENSE OF SELF

NEW THOUGHT PATTERNS

NEW CIRCUMSTANCES

NEW DESIRES

NEW ACTIONS

PLEASE NOTE... I AM NOT SAYING MEDITATION IS A MAGIC BULLET THAT WILL FIX ALL YOUR PROBLEMS! I PARTICIPATED IN MANY OTHER HEALING MODALITIES OVER THE COURSE OF MANY YEARS.

BUT I CREDIT MEDITATION FOR HELPING ME CREATE MORE SPACE WITHIN MYSELF TO MAKE MANY POSITIVE, BENEFICIAL CHANGES IN MY LIFE POSSIBLE.

EMBRACING MY FEMININE SIDE

*LOTS AND LOTS OF SELF-HELP BOOKS

CHANGING JOB & LIVING SITUATION

SUPPORTIVE RELATIONSHIPS

TALK THERAPY

MOVING MY BODY

*SOME OF MY FAVORITE SELF-HELP BOOKS ARE LISTED AT THE END OF THIS BOOK.

ANYWAY, ENOUGH **ABOUT ME!**

I AM SO EXCITED FOR YOUR
MEDITATION JOURNEY!

MY ADVICE IS PRESENTED AS
OFFERINGS AND INVITATION FOR
PLAYFUL EXPERIMENTATION.
THEY ARE NOT IRON-CLAD RULES.

PLEASE TAKE ONLY WHAT
RESONATES WITH YOU AND
CREATE YOUR OWN BEAUTIFUL,
UNIQUE JOURNEY.

MANY BLESSINGS TO YOU—AND
DON'T FORGET TO HAVE FUN! ✦

THERE IS NO RIGHT WAY TO MEDITATE

CONTRARY TO WHAT YOU MAY HAVE HEARD....

THERE ISN'T *JUST* ONE PERFECT, CORRECT, PURE WAY TO MEDITATE.

just as how there is no right way for a river to flow into an ocean

there are so many ways to meditate in order to expand your sense of inner peace and joy

MANY PEOPLE LIKE TO SIT IN A COMFORTABLE POSITION WITH THEIR EYES CLOSED

YOU CAN MEDITATE...

IN A CHAIR

ON THE FLOOR

OUTDOORS

IN A BIG GROUP

WITH MUSIC

OTHER PEOPLE LIKE TO MEDITATE

WHILE WALKING

WITH WIDE-OPEN EYES

do what you are most comfortable with

YOU CAN ALSO DECIDE WHAT YOU WANT TO FOCUS ON WHEN YOU ARE MEDITATING...

YOUR FAVORITE COLOR

I AM LOVE
mantras

AN IMAGE THAT BRINGS PEACE

YOUR BREATHING

YOUR DEITY/ DEITIES

INFINITY

INNER SILENCE

LOVE

PEACE *for all*

THE SOUND OF THE OCEAN

A FACE OF A LOVED ONE

SO THE BOTTOM LINE IS THIS:

MEDITATE EVERY DAY — EVEN IF IT MEANS YOU ARE PAYING EXTRA ATTENTION TO THE COLOR OF THE LEAVES FOR 30 SECONDS WHILE WALKING FROM THE POST OFFICE TO YOUR CAR

OR YOU FOCUS ON YOUR BREATHING FOR ONE MINUTE WHILE WAITING FOR YOUR APPOINTMENT AT THE DOCTOR'S OFFICE

SO NO MATTER HOW
BUSY YOU ARE...

SQUEEZE A LITTLE
MEDITATION INTO
YOUR EVERYDAY
SCHEDULE

AND EVERY DAY, YOUR
CAPACITY FOR PEACE,
JOY, AND COMPASSION
GROWS BY JUST A
LITTLE BIT

EXPERIMENT

MEDITATION CREATES SPACE IN YOUR LIFE. WHAT DO YOU DESIRE TO CALL IN WITHIN THE SPACES YOU ARE CREATING FOR YOURSELF?

IMAGINE FILLING THE EMPTY CIRCLE ABOVE
WITH EVERYTHING THAT YOUR HEART DESIRES—
NEW FEELINGS, NEW DESIRES, NEW THOUGHTS,
NEW OPPORTUNITIES, NEW ENERGY, NEW WAYS
OF BEING. LET YOUR IMAGINATION RUN WILD.
ANYTHING IS POSSIBLE!

JUST CREATE THE SPACE AND BE OPEN TO RECEIVE.

ATTENTION

PAYING ATTENTION IS HOW WE SHOW LOVE TO SOMEONE OR SOMETHING WE CARE ABOUT.

WE ARE CHOOSING TO GIVE THEM OUR LIMITED ATTENTION, TIME, ENERGY, AND SPACE OVER OTHER THINGS WE COULD BE GIVING THOSE THINGS TO.

WE NOTICE DIFFERENT THINGS ABOUT THE OBJECT OF OUR ATTENTION AND CAN RESPOND IN LOVING, CARING WAYS, AS OPPOSED TO NOT THINKING ABOUT THEM AT ALL OR THINKING VERY LITTLE ABOUT THEM.

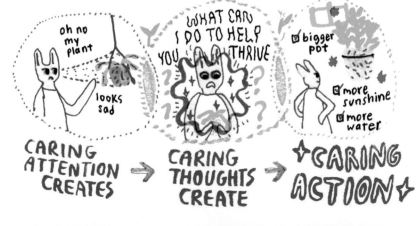

CARING ATTENTION CREATES → CARING THOUGHTS CREATE → ✦CARING ACTION✦

WHEN WE **GIVE** OUR FULL ATTENTION (NOTICE THE WORD "GIVE"... ATTENTION IS A PRECIOUS GIFT!), SOMEONE OR SOMETHING IS PRIORITIZED AS THE MOST IMPORTANT THING IN THE WHOLE ENTIRE WORLD, EVEN IF IT IS ONLY FOR THE ONE FLEETING MOMENT THAT THAT SOMEONE OR SOMETHING TAKES UP ALL OF YOUR TIME, ATTENTION, AND SPACE.

MANY OF US CAN PROBABLY THINK OF PAST INSTANCES WHEN RECEIVING LOVING ATTENTION FROM SOMEBODY TRULY FELT LIFE-CHANGING, MAYBE EVEN LIFE-SAVING.

AND SO, WHAT COULD POSSIBLY BE MORE IMPORTANT AS THE RECIPIENT OF YOUR PRECIOUS AND VALUABLE ATTENTION THAN YOU—YOUR INNER THOUGHTS, YOUR INNER WORLDS AND LANDSCAPES, YOUR BODY AND FEELINGS AND DESIRES, YOUR ENERGY, YOUR LIFE UNFOLDING BEFORE YOU MOMENT BY MOMENT?

SO WHAT DO YOU DO EXACTLY WHEN YOU MEDITATE?

SOME ASSUMPTIONS AND IDEAS YOU MAY HAVE ABOUT MEDITATION...

DO I NEED TO SIT PERFECTLY STILL AND SIT CROSS-LEGGED FOR 3 HOURS? (NO)

DO I NEED TO "THINK ABOUT NOTHING" AND COMPLETELY EMPTY MY THOUGHTS? (NO)

DO I NEED TO IDENTIFY AS A SPECIFIC RELIGION OR JOIN A SPIRITUAL GROUP? (NO)

ugh so boring

IF I DON'T REACH ENLIGHTENMENT AND I'M BORED/ IMPATIENT/ ANNOYED/ETC. AM I DOING IT WRONG? (NO)

WHETHER YOUR MEDITATION IS FOR ONE MINUTE, TEN MINUTES, ONE HOUR OR MORE... I PERSONALLY DEFINE MY OWN MEDITATION AND MINDFULNESS PRACTICE AS A CONTAINER OF TIME AND SPACE WHERE I AM PAYING ATTENTION.

MEDITATION IS PAYING ATTENTION

YOU CAN EVEN TRY IT RIGHT THIS MOMENT.

that's
it - _ seriously

YOU DON'T HAVE TO CLOSE YOUR EYES. YOU CAN KEEP YOUR EYES OPEN.

hmmm - okay

START TAKING A FEW DEEP BREATHS AND CONSCIOUSLY SLOW DOWN YOUR BREATHING. ALLOW YOURSELF TO SETTLE INTO A COMFORTABLE POSITION WHERE YOU CAN SIMPLY RELAX AND LOOSEN THE MUSCLES IN YOUR BODY.

inhale   exhale

AS YOUR BODY SETTLES INTO A SLOWED DOWN STATE OF BEING...

FOR ABOUT ONE WHOLE MINUTE SIMPLY NOTICE EVERYTHING AROUND YOU AND WITHIN YOU WITH ALL OF YOUR SENSES IN THIS PRESENT MOMENT.

SOUNDS

THE AIR AGAINST YOUR SKIN

THINGS TOUCHING YOUR SKIN

sensations in your body

YOUR EYEBALLS MOVING

THE TEXTURE OF THE SURFACE CONVEYING THIS TEXT

TEXTURES

COLORS

THOUGHTS FEELINGS IDEAS

WHAT?

WOW
BLINKING
IS WEIRD

ARF
ARF

BREATHING

ARF

CHIRP

CHIRP

SO... HOW WAS IT FOR YOU?

  - whoa

MAYBE PAYING ATTENTION FOR ONE FULL MINUTE WAS RELAXING FOR YOU. MAYBE YOU FELT BORED, IMPATIENT, ANNOYED, SUPER-DISTRACTED. MAYBE YOU FOUND IT INTERESTING. MAYBE YOU FELT ALL OF THE ABOVE, OR NONE OF THE ABOVE!

THERE ARE NO RIGHT OR WRONG RESPONSES OR REACTIONS IN MEDITATING.

FOR ALL OF THE MEDITATION EXERCISES IN THIS BOOK, BE CURIOUS AND NON-JUDGMENTAL, AND SIMPLY BE OPEN TO SEEING WHAT HAPPENS.

MINI MEDITATION EXPERIMENTS IN PAYING ATTENTION

TRY THE EXPERIMENT WE JUST DID EARLIER, BUT FOR FIVE MINUTES. SET A TIMER USING YOUR PHONE (OR A KITCHEN TIMER) AND FOR A FIVE-MINUTE CONTAINER OF TIME, SIMPLY SIT AND PAY ATTENTION TO THE **THINGS AROUND YOU** AND **WITHIN YOU.**

YOU CAN ALSO PAY ATTENTION TO *HOW* YOU ARE PAYING ATTENTION. HOW DOES IT FEEL IN YOUR MIND AND BODY WHEN YOU CONSCIOUSLY CHOOSE TO PAY ATTENTION?

NOTICE WHAT HAPPENS WHEN YOU GIVE SOMETHING YOUR FULL ATTENTION WITH LASER FOCUS, AS OPPOSED TO SHALLOW OR DISTRACTED ATTENTION.

LOVING ATTENTION EXPERIMENT

HOW DO YOU FEEL WHEN YOU RECEIVE LOVING, UNDIVIDED ATTENTION FROM SOMEONE WHO CARES ABOUT YOU, TRULY SEES YOU, ACCEPTS YOU FOR EXACTLY WHO YOU ARE?

IMAGINE SHOWERING AND BATHING YOURSELF IN AN OCEAN OF THIS UNCONDITIONAL LOVING ATTENTION. IMAGINE FEELING TRULY SEEN AND UNDERSTOOD.

IMAGINE FULLY RECEIVING THIS GIFT AND NOTICE HOW THAT FEELS IN YOUR BODY.

IMAGINE THAT YOU ARE FULLY RECEIVING THIS LOVING, ACCEPTING ATTENTION THAT YOU ARE ALSO FULLY GIVING TO YOURSELF.

LOVING ATTENTION EXPERIMENT
✦(AGAIN BUT DIFFERENT)✦

HOW DOES IT FEEL TO EFFORTLESSLY GIVE LOVING, UNDIVIDED ATTENTION TO SOMEONE YOU CARE ABOUT WHERE IT IS SO EFFORTLESS TO ACCEPT THEIR PRESENT STATE EXACTLY AS THEY ARE?

IMAGINE FULLY GIVING THAT UNDIVIDED, LOVING ATTENTION TO SOMEONE. NOW, IMAGINE GIVING THAT FULLY TO YOURSELF, FULLY RECEIVING WHAT YOU ARE ALSO GIVING.

FIELD OF ATTENTION

YES

MAYBE ?!

JOY

✦ LET YOUR EYES ROVE ACROSS THIS PAGE SPREAD!

NOTICE WHAT GRABS YOUR ATTENTION IMMEDIATELY,
WHAT YOUR EYES LINGER ON FOR LONGER,
WHAT DETAILS YOU DID NOT CATCH THE FIRST TIME,
ETC.

NOTICE ALL THE EMPTY SPACES AROUND THE
OBJECTS, TOO.

STRESS

SADNESS

BOO

Hi!

EXPERIMENT

SLOW DOWN

ENDINGS

PLEASURE

hi
you
are
loved

BEGINNINGS

⬦ TAKE NOTE OF HOW WHEN YOU PAY ATTENTION TO A SPECIFIC THING FOR LONGER THAN A MOMENT, YOU AMPLIFY IT IN YOUR MIND. ALSO, NOTICE HOW WHEN YOU MOVE YOUR ATTENTION AWAY FROM SOMETHING IT DISAPPEARS FROM YOUR PRESENT MIND SPACE BECAUSE YOUR ATTENTION HAS MOVED ONTO SOMETHING ELSE.

WHAT ARE YOU GIVING YOUR ATTENTION TO IN YOUR LIFE THAT DEPLETES YOUR ENERGY AND SENSE OF JOY?

ARE THERE WAYS YOU CAN DECREASE OR COMPLETELY ELIMINATE THE MENTAL AND PHYSICAL SPACE THEY TAKE UP IN YOUR LIFE?

WHAT ARE YOU GIVING YOUR ATTENTION TO THAT RAISES YOUR ENERGY AND EXPANDS YOUR SENSE OF JOY AND ALIVENESS?

ARE THERE WAYS YOU CAN INCREASE THOSE THINGS OR HOW MUCH TIME YOU SPEND ON THEM SO THEY TAKE UP MORE SPACE IN YOUR LIFE?

LISTENING MEDITATION

ONE OF MY FAVORITE WAYS TO GET INTO A MEDITATIVE STATE IS TO SIMPLY **LISTEN.**

RIGHT THIS MOMENT, TURN DOWN THE VOLUME OF YOUR INNER DIALOGUE. REALLY **LISTEN.** CAN YOU PICK UP AT LEAST THREE DIFFERENT LAYERS OF SOUND?

NOTICE ALSO THE GAPS BETWEEN SOUNDS
WHEN THERE ARE NO SOUNDS—WHICH IS
ALSO ITS OWN SOUND, TOO!

CAN YOU ALSO HEAR THE LAYER OF SILENCE
THAT IS ALWAYS PRESENT UNDERNEATH
ALL LAYERS OF SOUND?

YOU CAN ALSO DO A
LISTENING MEDITATION
NOT ONLY FOR EXTERNAL
SOUNDS, BUT ALSO FOR
INTERNAL SOUNDS:

THE SOUNDS OF YOUR
OWN INNER THOUGHTS
AND DIALOGUE.

HOW TO LISTEN TO THE SPACES BETWEEN YOUR THOUGHTS

STEP ONE:

LISTEN TO
YOUR THOUGHTS

STEP TWO:

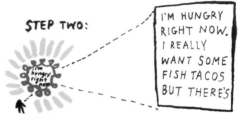

IMAGINE YOUR THOUGHTS BEING
TRANSCRIBED ON A GIANT SCREEN
AS YOU ARE THINKING THEM

STEP THREE:

NOTICE
THE SPACES
BETWEEN
YOUR THOUGHTS

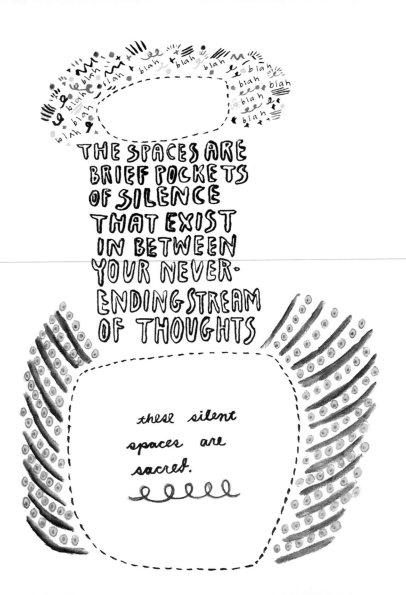

THE SPACES ARE BRIEF POCKETS OF SILENCE THAT EXIST IN BETWEEN YOUR NEVER-ENDING STREAM OF THOUGHTS

these silent spaces are sacred.

HAVING MORE **SPACE** IN YOUR THOUGHTS MEANS YOU HAVE MORE ROOM FOR YOUR **TRUE ESSENCE** TO SHINE THROUGH

SO START LISTENING TO THE SILENT SPACES IN YOUR THOUGHTS AND ENJOY THE WELLS OF PEACE THAT EXIST WITHIN THEM.

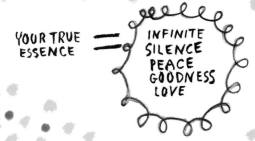

YOUR TRUE
ESSENCE

INFINITE
SILENCE
PEACE
GOODNESS
LOVE

BREATHING

I LIKE TO PAY ATTENTION TO MY BREATH WHEN I AM MEDITATING.

BREATHING IN THROUGH MY NOSE... FEELING THE AIR GO INTO MY BODY DOWN MY THROAT, FEELING MY CHEST AND LUNGS EXPAND... THEN RELEASING AIR FROM MY LUNGS, UP MY THROAT AND OUT THROUGH MY MOUTH AS I EXHALE.

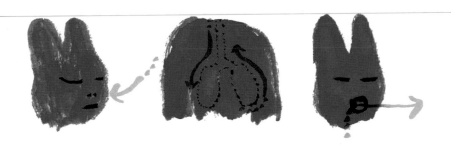

AND STARTING THE CYCLE AGAIN ONCE MORE.

YOU CAN DO A MINI
BREATHING MEDITATION
RIGHT NOW.

SETTLE INTO A COMFORTABLE
POSITION AND TAKE THREE
SLOW, MINDFUL BREATHS.
BE ATTENTIVE TO EVERY MOMENT
AND SENSATION AS YOU COMPLETE
THREE FULL CYCLES OF DEEP, MINDFUL
BREATHING.

inhale
(hhhhhhh)
5 4 3 2 1

(haaaaaa)
exhale
5 4 3 2 1

inhale   exhale

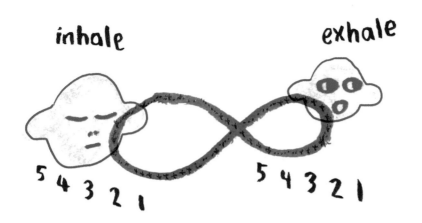

5 4 3 2 1   5 4 3 2 1

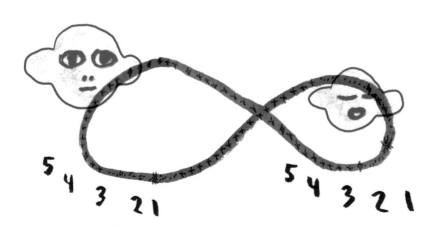

5 4 3 21   5 4 3 2 1

GREAT JOB!
YOU JUST DID A MEDITATION!

TAKING *SLOOOO O OW* DEEP MINDFUL BREATHS, ESPECIALLY WHEN YOU ARE FEELING STRESSED OR ANXIOUS, IS A VERY SIMPLE AND EFFECTIVE WAY TO LET YOUR BODY KNOW THAT **YOU ARE SAFE** AND NOT IN DANGER.

AS AN EXTRA, YOU CAN ALSO TAP ON YOUR COLLAR BONES WITH YOUR FINGERS AND HEAVILY PAT THE TOP OF YOUR THIGHS IF YOU ARE SITTING DOWN TO FURTHER INCREASE YOUR PHYSICAL SENSE OF FEELING GROUNDED.

OTHER MEDITATION EXPERIMENTS FOR BREATHING

WHENEVER YOU ARE FEELING STRESSED, IMAGINE THE FEELINGS OF STRESS TAKING UP SPACE IN YOUR BODY AS HEAVY BLACK CLOUDS...

DRAW THEM UP INTO YOUR LUNGS WITH A LONG, DEEP INHALE...

EXHALE THEM OUT OF YOUR BODY AS SPARKLING WHITE LIGHT.

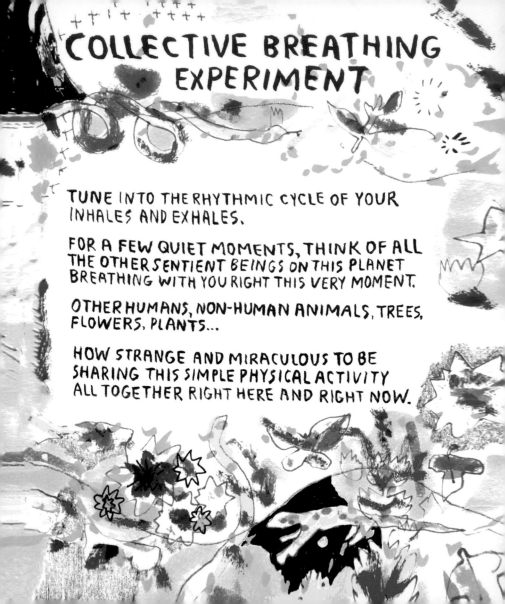

COLLECTIVE BREATHING EXPERIMENT

TUNE INTO THE RHYTHMIC CYCLE OF YOUR INHALES AND EXHALES.

FOR A FEW QUIET MOMENTS, THINK OF ALL THE OTHER SENTIENT BEINGS ON THIS PLANET BREATHING WITH YOU RIGHT THIS VERY MOMENT.

OTHER HUMANS, NON-HUMAN ANIMALS, TREES, FLOWERS, PLANTS...

HOW STRANGE AND MIRACULOUS TO BE SHARING THIS SIMPLE PHYSICAL ACTIVITY ALL TOGETHER RIGHT HERE AND RIGHT NOW.

SOMETIMES IT'S OKAY IF THE ONLY THING YOU DID TODAY WAS BREATHE

and
every time
you breathe
in, a new
idea is
born

and

every time
you breathe
out, an old
grievance is
released

BREATHE IN

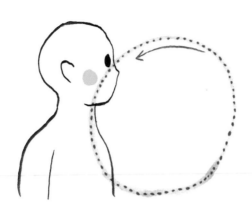

BREATHE OUT

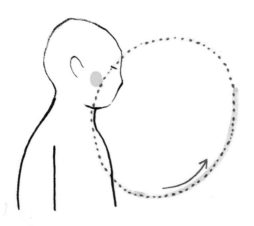

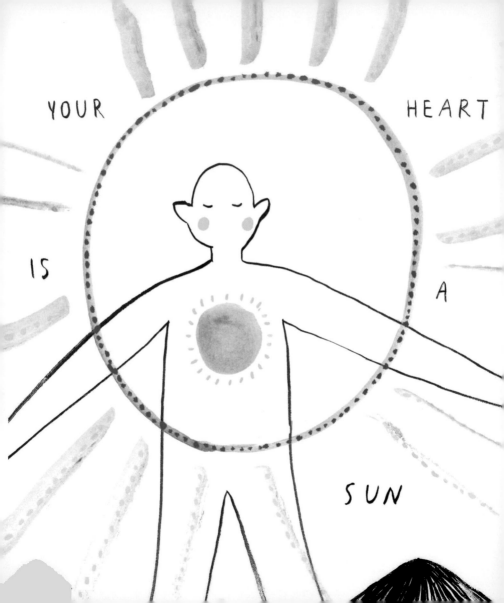

EXPERIMENT

BREATHE IN A COLOR
INTO YOUR BODY.

LET IT SWIRL AROUND
IN YOUR LUNGS, AND THEN
BREATHE IT OUT.

EXPERIMENT WITH
DIFFERENT COLORS FOR
DIFFERENT EFFECTS ON
YOUR MOOD.

BODY

YOUR BODY IS AN ALWAYS-EVOLVING, DYNAMIC, AND ALIVE
ECOSYSTEM THAT IS ALWAYS CHANGING AND IS ALWAYS
GOING THROUGH ITS OWN UNIQUE RHYTHMS, SEASONS,
CYCLES, AND NEEDS THAT CHANGE OVER TIME.

WE LEARN SO MUCH WHEN WE CHOOSE TO PAUSE AND PAY ATTENTION TO OUR BODIES. OUR BODIES CARRY SO MUCH WISDOM AND IMPORTANT MESSAGES!

WE CAN LISTEN TO OUR BODIES AS WE WOULD TO A DEAR AND BELOVED FRIEND WHEN WE TAKE THE TIME TO MEDITATE.

A SIMPLE BODY MEDITATION

YOU CAN DO THIS SITTING OR LYING DOWN.

DO WHATEVER IS MOST COMFORTABLE WITH YOU.

CLOSE YOUR EYES IF YOU WANT TO

TAKE A FEW SLOW, MINDFUL BREATHS TO GET SETTLED INTO THIS PRESENT MOMENT.

INHALE... EXHALE... INHALE... EXHALE...

STARTING FROM THE TOP OF YOUR HEAD AND WORKING YOUR WAY DOWN TO YOUR TOES, DO AN ATTENTION SCAN OF THE ENTIRE LENGTH OF YOUR BODY.

WITH NON-JUDGMENT AND ACCEPTANCE, SIMPLY TAKE NOTE OF WHAT SENSATIONS AND FEELINGS ARE PRESENT IN DIFFERENT AREAS OF YOUR BODY. WHAT FEELS TIGHT, CONSTRICTED? WHAT FEELS LOOSE AND RELAXED? WHAT FEELS ACHEY? PLEASURABLE? NEUTRAL?

YOU CAN PLACE HANDS ON YOUR BODY WHERE IT FEELS GOOD AND COMFORTABLE.

YOU CAN ALSO BREATHE LOVING, COMFORTING ENERGY INTO PARTS OF YOUR BODY THAT FEEL LIKE THEY NEED EXTRA ATTENTION.

SOMETIMES IT HELPS ME TO THINK OF MY BODY AS A LOVABLE SQUISHY BLOBBY SENTIENT BEING THAT IS SO LOVABLE SIMPLY FOR BEING ALIVE AND HAS VERY SIMPLE NEEDS. AND I WISH ONLY THE BEST THINGS FOR THEM AND IT IS MY RESPONSIBILITY TO MAKE SURE THEY ARE HAPPY, HEALTHY, AND HAVE ALL THEIR NEEDS MET.

91

ALIVENESS MEDITATION

① INHALE AND EXHALE FOR A FEW MINDFUL CYCLES

② FEEL THE ALIVENESS WITHIN YOU THAT IS THE SAME ALIVENESS FLOWING THROUGH OTHER HUMAN: PLANTS, ANIMALS, THE OCEAN, THE MOUNTAINS, AND THE STARS.

③ IMAGINE THAT YOU ARE BATHING IN AN OCEAN OF SPARKLING VIBRANT ALIVENESS THAT WAKES UP EVERY CELL OF YOUR BODY.

a simple illustrated guided meditation

① SIT IN A COMFORTABLE POSITION.

② FEEL THE WEIGHT OF THE AIR AROUND YOU.

③ FEEL THE SURFACE OF YOUR OWN SKIN.

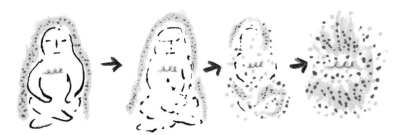

④ NOW IMAGINE THAT A MAGICAL ERASER IS ERASING THE OUTLINE OF YOUR BEING...

⑤ UNTIL THERE IS NO BOUNDARY BETWEEN YOU AND THE REST OF THE UNIVERSE.

93

FEELING YOUR BODY FOR THE FIRST TIME

IMAGINE THAT YOU ARE A FRIENDLY EXTRATERRESTRIAL BEING CURIOUS ABOUT THE HUMAN EXPERIENCE.

YOU STEP INTO THIS HUMAN VESSEL THAT IS YOUR BODY. **WOW!** EVERYTHING IS SO STRANGE AND INTERESTING AND FASCINATING AND NEW... BREATHING, BLINKING, WALKING, FEELING TOUCH, HAVING A HEART BEATING IN YOUR CHEST.

GO OUTSIDE AND MOVE THROUGH THE WORLD AT YOUR OWN PACE AS THOUGH YOU ARE EXPERIENCING IT ALL FOR THE VERY FIRST TIME.

DOING NOTHING MEDITATION

LET YOUR BODY DO NOTHING.

LIKE YOU ARE A SEED PLANTED INTO THE EARTH. THE EARTH PRESSES ONTO YOU LIKE THE MOST COMFORTING BLANKET THAT MAKES YOU FEEL LIKE THE MOST SAFE AND PROTECTED TENDER BEING IN THE UNIVERSE.

YOUR ONLY JOB IS TO SIMPLY REST, RELEASE ALL CONSTRICTION IN YOUR BODY, AND TRUST THAT THE MAGIC WITHIN YOU AND AROUND YOU WILL GROW YOU INTO WHOEVER YOU ARE MEANT TO BECOME.

DOING NOTHING IS NOT REALLY "DOING NOTHING!"

WHEN YOU ARE DOING NOTHING, YOU ARE LETTING YOURSELF REST. YOU ARE GIVING YOUR MIND AND BODY AND SPIRIT BREATHING ROOM TO PROCESS THOUGHTS, EMOTIONS, IDEAS, INFORMATION.

YOU CAN LET YOUR MIND WANDER FREELY AND DAYDREAM.

YOU ARE DIGESTING THE EVENTS OF YOUR DAY AND INTEGRATING NEW INFORMATION INTO YOUR LIFE.

YOU ARE CATCHING UP WITH YOURSELF AS YOU WOULD WITH A DEAR FRIEND OR LOVED ONE YOU HAVEN'T SEEN IN A BIT.

YOU ARE BEING. YOU ARE BEING YOUR WONDERFUL PRECIOUS SELF WHO IS SO LOVABLE SIMPLY FOR BEING ALIVE.

sorry i can't hang out tonight i got like 10 things going on i'm soooo busy

1. REST
2. DAYDREAM
3. LOOK AT CLOUDS
4. BREATHE
5. DIGEST 6. CHILL
7. RELAX 8. PROCESS LIFE
9. BE 10. EXIST

HOW TO JUST BE

STEP ONE:
FEEL YOURSELF
BREATHING

STEP TWO:
FEEL THE LIGHT
PRESSURE OF
YOUR HEART
BEATING AGAINST
YOUR RIBCAGE

STEP THREE:
FEEL THE EMPTY
SPACE BEHIND
YOUR EYEBALLS

STEP FOUR:
FEEL YOU AS
JUST YOU
BEING YOU
AND BE OKAY
WITH IT

THOUGHTS

✦ MEDITATION HELPS YOU PAY ATTENTION.

✦ MEDITATION HELPS YOU PAY ATTENTION TO HOW YOU PAY ATTENTION.

✦ WHEN YOU START PAYING ATTENTION TO YOUR THOUGHTS, YOU START GAINING NEW INSIGHTS ABOUT YOURSELF.

✦ AS YOU OBSERVE YOUR THOUGHTS WITH NON-JUDGMENT AND COMPASSION, YOU BEGIN TO CREATE A LITTLE EXTRA SPACE, A LITTLE EXTRA PAUSE BETWEEN YOUR THOUGHTS AND YOUR ACTIONS WHERE YOU GET TO DECIDE FOR YOURSELF:

✦ DOES THIS THOUGHT SERVE ME?

✦ YES OR NO?

THOUGHTS ABOUT STRESS

THOUGHTS ABOUT PEOPLE I LOVE

THOUGHTS ABOUT THOUGHTS????

BLAH BLAH

THOUGHT ABOUT CUTE PUPPIES

THOUGHTS ABOUT SNACKS

GARBAGE THO

THOUGHTS ABOUT MY ENEM

INTERRU THOUG

BRILLIA IDEA THOUGH SAYING

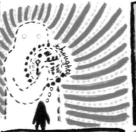

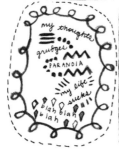

BEING A SILENT WITNESS TO YOUR THOUGHTS TURNS WHAT FEELS LIKE IRREFUTABLE REALITY INTO WHAT IT REALLY IS — A TEMPORARY STATE OF A THOUGHT FORM THAT YOU ARE EXPERIENCING ONLY FOR THIS MOMENT.

BEFORE WE PROCEED FURTHER... A VERY IMPORTANT MESSAGE

i'm fine
it's not raining
i'm not sad at all
i can change my thoughts

PLEASE DO NOT USE THOUGHTWORK (THE PRACTICE OF MINDFULLY OBSERVING AND QUESTIONING YOUR THOUGHTS) AGAINST YOU, SUCH AS DENYING YOUR OWN REALITY OR INVALIDATING YOUR OWN TRUTH. THESE EXPERIMENTS IDEALLY WILL CREATE MORE SPACIOUSNESS AND OPENNESS AND CHOICES FOR HOW YOU MENTALLY INTERPRET YOUR OWN LIFE EVENTS AND EXPERIENCES. MAYBE FOR SOME SITUATIONS, THOUGHTWORK IS NOT THE BEST OPTION, AND ANOTHER COPING STRATEGY MAKES MORE SENSE. PLEASE SEEK PROFESSIONAL HELP AND GUIDANCE IF THOUGHTS ARE TOO OVERWHELMING FOR YOU TO HANDLE ON YOUR OWN.

IMAGINE THAT YOUR THOUGHTS ARE LEAVES FLOATING DOWNSTREAM ON THE SURFACE OF A RIVER. SIMPLY ALLOW THEM TO DRIFT BY WITHOUT GETTING ATTACHED TO ANY SINGLE LEAF.

IMAGINE THAT YOUR THOUGHTS ARE A PARADE OF DIFFERENT PERSONALITIES PASSING BY. EVERY THOUGHT IS REPRESENTED BY A DIFFERENT CHARACTER SAYING THE THOUGHT.

YOU GET TO DECIDE WHETHER OR NOT YOU TRUST THE THOUGHT-CHARACTER TELLING THEIR THOUGHT TO YOU.

YOU CAN IMAGINE HIGHLIGHTING THE TEXT OF
YOUR THOUGHTS AND TRANSLATING THEM INTO
GIBBERISH (OR SHAPES, OR ANIMALS.)

My friend hasn't texted back yet
oh no they hate me now

My friend hasn't texted back yet
oh no they hate me now

TRANSLATE

YOU CAN IMAGINE THAT YOUR THOUGHTS
ARE AN IMAGE ON YOUR PHONE THAT YOU CAN
ZOOM WAY OUT OF TO SEE THE BIGGER PICTURE
OR ZOOM WAY IN UNTIL ALL YOU SEE ARE
PIXELS AND GRADIENTS.

SKY MEDITATION

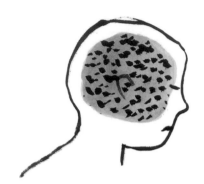

YOU ARE NOT

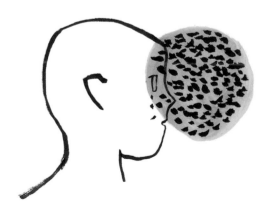

YOUR THOUGHTS

THEY ARE CLOUDS

PASSING BY

AND YOU ARE

THE SKY

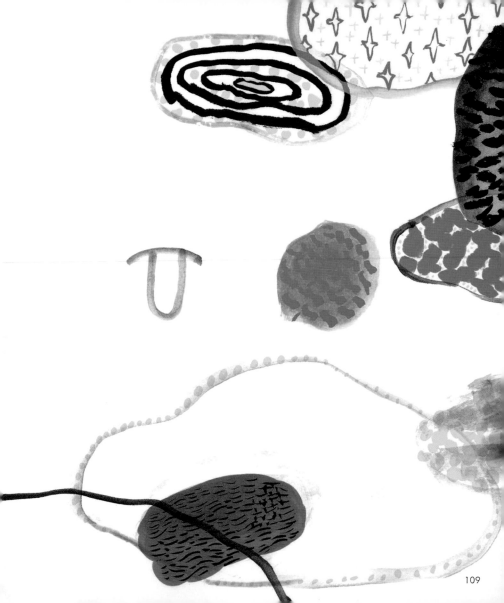

RIGHT THIS MOMENT THERE IS A SELF-DEPRECATING THOUGHT WITHIN ME

RIGHT THIS MOMENT THERE IS A SELF-AFFIRMING THOUGHT WITHIN ME

RIGHT THIS MOMENT THERE IS A THOUGHT ABOUT DINNER WITHIN ME

RIGHT THIS MOMENT THERE IS A THOUGHT ABOUT A CUTE DOG WITHIN ME

RIGHT THIS MOMENT THERE IS A SELF-AWARE THOUGHT ABOUT THE NATURE OF THOUGHTS WITHIN ME

RIGHT THIS MOMENT THERE
ARE THOUGHTS WITHIN ME

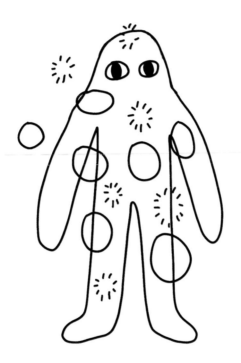

AND
ALSO SPACE AROUND
THE THOUGHTS WITHIN ME

I ONCE HEARD EMOTION REFERRED TO AS E-MOTION - E(nergy in) MOTION. EMOTIONS ARE MEANT TO MOVE. WHEN EMOTIONS ARE FULLY FELT, THEY GET TO SHIFT, MOVE THROUGH YOUR BODY, AND BE RELEASED THROUGH BREATH, MOVEMENT, AND/OR VOICE.

WHEN WE AVOID FEELING OUR FEELINGS, THEY REMAIN STUCK IN OUR BODIES AND DO NOT HAVE THE SPACE TO FLOW INTO SOMETHING ELSE.

JUST AS HOW WE CAN BE A SILENT WITNESS TO OUR THOUGHTS AND INNER DIALOGUE. WE CAN ALSO BE A SILENT WITNESS TO OUR FEELINGS. WE CAN BE COMPASSIONATE, ASK QUESTIONS, AND ACCEPT AND AFFIRM THEIR EXISTENCE.

INSTEAD OF LABELING FEELINGS AS "GOOD" OR "BAD" OR HAVING SECONDARY FEELINGS ABOUT PRIMARY FEELINGS (EXAMPLE: I AM MAD AT MYSELF THAT I AM STILL SAD), WE CAN ASK WITH CURIOSITY: "WHAT IS THIS FEELING TRYING TO COMMUNICATE TO ME RIGHT NOW?"

hey let's talk

OUR FEELINGS DON'T ALWAYS FIT INTO NEAT CATEGORIES.

HOW DO YOU FEEL TODAY?

SOMETIMES IT HELPS ME TO SEE FEELINGS AS MULTILAYERED, MULTIDIMENSIONAL EXPERIENCES — COMPLEX ECOSYSTEMS OR LANDSCAPES, PLANETS WITH SHIFTING WEATHER PATTERNS, COLOR FIELDS WITH OVERLAPPING HUES AND PATTERNS AND TEXTURES, FANTASTICAL CREATURES THAT SHIFT AND MORPH INTO MANY DIFFERENT FORMS.

HOW DO YOU FEEL TODAY?

VISUALIZE YOUR
OWN UNIQUE
FEELING-STATE
HERE

LOVING ATTENTION TURNED INWARD TOWARDS YOUR EMOTIONAL STATE CAN REVEAL, WITH COMPASSION AND PATIENCE, THE MANY LAYERS OF FEELINGS AND DESIRES HIDDEN BENEATH YOUR PRIMARY EXPERIENCE OF THE ORIGINAL FEELING.

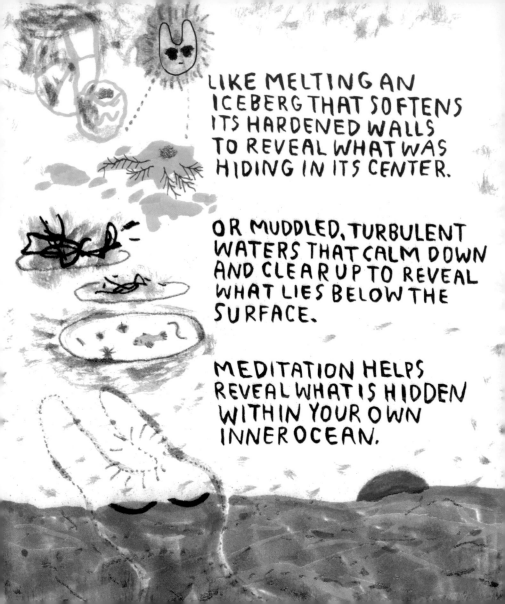

LIKE MELTING AN ICEBERG THAT SOFTENS ITS HARDENED WALLS TO REVEAL WHAT WAS HIDING IN ITS CENTER.

OR MUDDLED, TURBULENT WATERS THAT CALM DOWN AND CLEAR UP TO REVEAL WHAT LIES BELOW THE SURFACE.

MEDITATION HELPS REVEAL WHAT IS HIDDEN WITHIN YOUR OWN INNER OCEAN.

A MINDFUL GUIDE TO HOLDING SPACE FOR YOUR FEELINGS

1. ACKNOWLEDGE THE TRUTH OF WHAT YOU ARE FEELING AND EXPERIENCING.

i am feeling

_____

(tired. grief, rage, hopeless, defeated, blah, etc.)

IT IS ALSO OKAY IF YOU DON'T KNOW HOW YOU FEEL

2. TAKE A MOMENT TO FEEL WHERE IN YOUR BODY YOU ARE FEELING YOUR EMOTIONS.

my chest?

3. GIVE A COLOR, VIBRATION, TEXTURE, OR SHAPE TO YOUR EMOTIONS. HOW WOULD YOU DESCRIBE THEM IN THOSE TERMS?

like squiggly, oily, black coils laced with bolts of lightning bouncing around, making me feel uneasy

4. BREATHE MINDFULLY AND DEEPLY INTO THE PART OF YOUR BODY THAT IS HOLDING YOUR EMOTIONS. MAYBE PLACE YOUR HAND OVER THAT PART OF YOUR BODY. THERE IS NO PRESSURE TO CHANGE OR FIX OR ANALYZE WHAT YOU ARE FEELING.

5. ASK YOURSELF: WHAT DO YOU NEED RIGHT NOW IN ORDER TO FEEL SAFE AND SUPPORTED? WHAT WOULD FEEL GOOD FOR YOU RIGHT NOW? IT CAN BE SIMPLE: A WALK, A NAP, A SNACK, A GLASS OF WATER, REACHING OUT TO A FRIEND, ETC.

6. VALIDATE WHAT YOU ARE FEELING. YOU DON'T HAVE TO MINIMIZE IT, FIX IT, DENY IT, OR RUSH TO FIND THE SILVER LINING OR IMPORTANT LESSON.

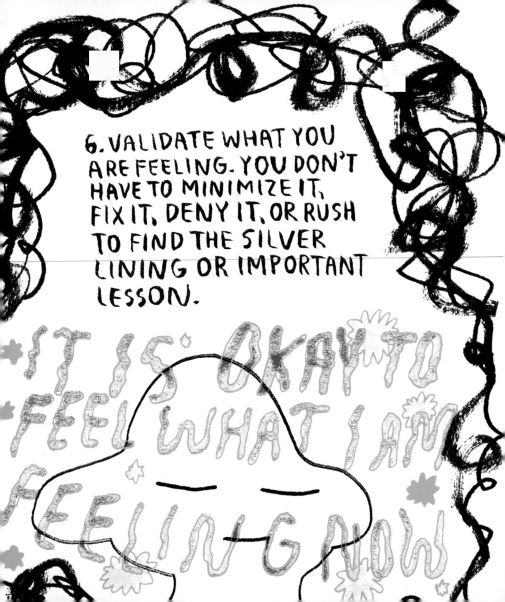

IT IS OKAY TO FEEL WHAT I AM FEELING NOW

8. THANK YOURSELF FOR TAKING THE TIME TO HOLD SPACE FOR YOUR OWN FEELINGS AND KNOW THAT THIS IS A PRACTICE YOU CAN RETURN TO AGAIN AND AGAIN. YOU CAN ALSO DO THIS WITH LOVED ONES, A THERAPIST, AND OTHERS YOU FEEL SAFE WITH (WITH THEIR CONSENT!). BONUS: GIVE YOURSELF A BIG HUG!

thank you, me

you're welcome, me

DESIRE,
INTENTION,
AND
IMAGINATION

MEDITATION IS GREAT FOR FINDING THE PEACE OF MIND TO ACCEPT CIRCUMSTANCES BEYOND YOUR CONTROL. I'VE FOUND THAT THROUGH DAILY MEDITATION PRACTICE IT GETS EASIER TO CREATE SPACE IN YOUR BRAIN TO CHOOSE YOUR REACTION AND ATTITUDE TOWARDS EXTERNAL EVENTS INSTEAD OF GETTING SWEPT UP BY HABITUAL AUTOMATIC RESPONSES (WHICH SOMETIMES MAY NOT BE THE HEALTHIEST COPING MECHANISM).

IN ADDITION TO CONSCIOUSLY CHOOSING OUR REACTIONS TO THINGS, WE CAN ALSO GENERATE OUR OWN THOUGHTS, FEELINGS, DESIRES, IDEAS, AND VISIONS FOR THE CIRCUMSTANCES AND EXPERIENCES WE WISH TO CREATE, AND WHERE WE WANT TO END UP IN OUR ONGOING LIFE JOURNEY.

WHERE TO?

THIS IS WHY IT IS IMPORTANT TO PAY ATTENTION TO OUR DESIRES—WHICH TELL US WHAT MAKES US FEEL THE MOST ALIVE AND THE MOST RADIANT VERSION OF OURSELVES—HOW IT WOULD FEEL PHYSICALLY, EMOTIONALLY, SPIRITUALLY, RELATIONALLY TO MANIFEST THESE DESIRES INTO REALITY.

THIS IS ALSO WHY IT IS IMPORTANT TO SET AN INTENTION, TOO—WHICH IS AN ENERGETIC COMMITTMENT TO SEE THIS DESIRE THROUGH INSTEAD OF LETTING IT KNOCK AROUND IN YOUR BRAIN WHILE YOU DO NOTHING ABOUT IT.

THIS IS WHERE **IMAGINATION** COMES IN. WHEN WE VISUALIZE OURSELVES GOING ON THE JOURNEY AND REACHING OUR DESIRED DESTINATION, IT MAKES IT MORE POSSIBLE IN OUR MINDS.

IT GETS EASIER THEN TO TAKE SPECIFIC ACTION STEPS BECAUSE IT FEELS MORE REAL AND PLAUSIBLE INSTEAD OF A FARAWAY FANTASY.

DESIRE IS THE

SPARK OF INSPIRATION THAT IS FUEL FOR YOUR JOURNEY TO MAKE IT HAPPEN.

INTENTION IS

CREATING THE PATHWAY THAT WILL TAKE YOU TO YOUR DESIRED DESTINATION, MAKING AN INTERNAL COMMITMENT TO YOURSELF THAT YOU WILL MAKE THE EFFORT TO TAKE STEPS FORWARD.

LET'S GO!!!

IT'S OKAY THAT YOU DON'T KNOW EVERY STEP

EXPERIMENTS IN DESIRE, INTENTION, AND IMAGINATION

WHAT ARE YOUR DESIRES?

ASK YOURSELF THIS. MAKE SPACE FOR YOUR ANSWERS. LET YOUR **DESIRES** TAKE UP SPACE IN YOUR MIND, BODY, AND SPIRIT. WRITE DOWN AT LEAST 10 DESIRES—NO MATTER HOW BIG OR SMALL OR MUNDANE OR "UNREALISTIC".

THE ONLY RULE — THIS DESIRE MUST GIVE YOU A JOLT OF VISCERAL **EXCITEMENT** IN YOUR BODY!

PICK 2-3 DESIRES THAT GIVE THE MOST ELECTRIC CHARGE IN YOUR BODY AND HEART.

A HOUSE... IN THE WOODS?

USING YOUR IMAGINATION, HAVE FUN DESIRING YOUR DESIRES, IMAGINING IN FULL SENSORY DETAIL HOW AWESOME IT WOULD FEEL TO MAKE IT ALL COME TRUE.

ASK YOUR FUTURE SELF FOR ADVICE ON HOW TO MOVE FORWARD WITH THIS DESIRE. WHAT SMALL ACTION STEP CAN YOU TAKE TODAY?

SET AN INTENTION TO MAKE THIS DESIRE COME TRUE.

✸ REMIND YOURSELF THAT YOU ALREADY KNOW HOW TO TAP INTO YOUR DESIRES, SET AN INTENTION, AND USE YOUR IMAGINATION TO TAKE ACTION STEPS TO MAKE YOUR DESIRES COME TRUE.

I DESIRE TO EAT PIZZA

MY INTENT IS TO EAT PIZZA TONIGHT

I WILL RESEARCH THE BEST PIZZA IN TOWN AND ORDER FROM THEM

SUCCESS

✸ PRACTICE DESIRING AND VISUALIZING BIGGER DESIRES FOR YOURSELF. LET YOUR IMAGINATION RUN WILD! PLAY AROUND WITH BIG GENERAL DREAMS AS WELL AS SUPER-SPECIFIC SCENARIOS. RELEASE THE IDEA THAT YOU HAVE TO "DESERVE" MANIFESTING A DESIRE. IT IS OKAY TO RECEIVE AND WANT MORE.

I DESIRE MORE TRAVEL?

I DESIRE TAKING A TWO WEEK VACATION

I DESIRE SPENDING A YEAR TRAVELING THE WORLD WITH MY BEST FRIENDS!

DESIRE INTENTION IMAGINATION CHEAT SHEET

- **DOWNLOAD YOUR DESIRES** PAY ATTENTION TO DESIRES THAT FEEL THE MOST POTENT AND EXCITING.

- **FEEL IN YOUR BODY THE EXCITEMENT OF THIS DESIRE**

- **VISUALIZE IN FULL, SENSORY, EMOTIONAL, ENERGETIC DETAIL HOW IT WOULD FEEL FOR FUTURE YOU TO FULLY ENJOY MANIFESTING YOUR DESIRES**

- **SET AN INTENTION THAT YOU WILL TAKE NECESSARY ACTION TO MAKE THIS DESIRE COME TRUE**

- **VISUALIZE YOURSELF GOING THROUGH ALL THE ACTION STEPS**

- **LISTEN TO MESSAGES AND CLUES FROM THE UNIVERSE AND ACT ACCORDINGLY**

- **ENJOY THE JOURNEY AND DON'T FORGET TO HAVE FUN!**

WE ARE A PART OF EVERYTHING

THERE IS EVERYTHING WITHIN US

THERE IS AN OCEAN WITHIN ME

I AM WITHIN THE OCEAN

THERE IS A FLOWER WITHIN ME

I AM WITHIN EVERY FLOWER

THERE IS A DANCING STAR WITHIN ME

I AM WITHIN EVERY DANCING STAR

YOU ARE WITHIN ME

I AM WITHIN YOU

MINI INTERCONNECTED WEB EXPERIMENT

SIT OR LIE DOWN COMFORTABLY IN A QUIET PLACE.
TAKE DEEP INHALES AND EXHALES. CLOSE YOUR EYES
(IF YOU WANT), AND, AS YOU SETTLE INTO YOUR BODY, FEEL
INTO ALL THE DIFFERENT WAYS YOU ARE CONNECTED
TO THE REST OF THE WORLD ALL AROUND YOU— YOUR
RELATIONSHIPS, YOUR FAVORITE ANIMALS, ANCESTORS,
NATURE, SUNSHINE, AIR, STARS, THE OCEAN, ETC.

FEEL HOW THIS VIBRANT WEB OF ALIVENESS CONNECTS
US ALL TOGETHER IN ONE EXPANSIVE TAPESTERY.
FEEL ALL THE CONNECTIONS RUNNING THROUGH
YOUR BODY CONNECTING YOU TO EVERYTHING AND
EVERYONE.

A SPECIAL INTERCONNECTED
WEB EXPERIMENT ONLY FOR
SENTIENT BEINGS WHO ARE
READING THIS BOOK
RIGHT THIS MOMENT...

ARE YOU READY?

TURN THE PAGE TO FIND OUT MORE...

SEND OUT INTO THIS SHARED ENERGETIC WEB SOMETHING GOOD THAT YOU WOULD WANT FOR SOMEONE TO RECEIVE

SOME IDEAS...
- ✦ THE SMELL OF ORANGES
- ✦ A WARM PINK GLOW OF SOFT TENDERNESS
- ✦ A CALMING COLOR AND THE SOUND OF RAIN
- ✦ AN EXCITING SPARKLE

NOW CLOSE YOUR EYES AND **RECEIVE** SOMETHING GOOD THAT SOMEONE ON THIS SHARED VORTEX HAS ALREADY SENT FOR SOMEONE ELSE

SEND THEM AN ENERGETIC *THANK YOU*

REPEAT AS OFTEN AS NEEDED

INTERCONNECTED WEB EXPERIMENT

SIT DOWN / LIE DOWN COMFORTABLY AND CLOSE YOUR EYES. TUNE INTO YOUR BREATHING, TAKING SLOW DEEP INHALES AND EXHALES.

THINK ABOUT ALL THE PLANTS, TREES, AND GREENERY THAT GIFT YOU THE OXYGEN YOU NEED IN ORDER FOR YOU TO STAY ALIVE.

WITH EVERY INHALE AND EXHALE, SEND OUT GRATITUDE TO THE PLANTS ON THIS PLANET.

CONTINUE THIS FOR A FEW CYCLES, FEELING INTO THE SYMBIOTIC RELATIONSHIP WE ARE ALL IN TOGETHER, GIVING AND RECEIVING AND SHARING ALL TOGETHER THIS VERY PRESENT MOMENT.

NOW IMAGINE 3-5 OF YOUR CLOSEST RELATIONSHIPS.

FEEL INTO HOW MUCH YOU LOVE AND CHERISH THEM. AND ALL THE LOVE THAT THEY BRING INTO YOUR LIFE. AND ALL THE WAYS YOU ARE ALL BOUND TOGETHER ACROSS TIME AND SPACE. FULLY RECEIVE THEIR LOVE WITH EVERY INHALE. SEND THEM YOUR LOVE AND GRATITUDE WITH EVERY EXHALE.

NOW FEEL INTO PEOPLE IN YOUR GREATER
COMMUNITY WHO BRING GOOD THINGS INTO
YOUR LIFE. FULLY RECEIVE THEIR CARE WITH
EVERY INHALE. WITH EVERY EXHALE, SEND
GRATITUDE TO THEM FOR CONTRIBUTING
TO YOUR CARE.

WHAT ARE YOUR
HOPES, DREAMS, AND
WISHES FOR OUR
SHARED WEB? SEND
THEM OUT INTO THE
UNIVERSE.

WE CAN ALL HELP
MAKE EACH OTHER'S
DEEPEST DREAMS
AND WILDEST DESIRES
COME TRUE.

WE CAN MAKE NEW
SHAPES, VIBRATIONS, COLORS,
STRUCTURES IN OUR SHARED
WEB WITH OUR IDEAS,
IMAGINATIONS, SHARED
DREAMS, AND ACTIONS.

SEND AN ENERGETIC HELLO TO OUR INTERCONNECTED WEB.

LISTEN IN YOUR HEART FOR THE ENERGETIC HELLO BEING SENT BACK TO YOU.

THIS BOOK IS
DEDICATED TO YOU,
MY FELLOW WAVE
IN THE COSMIC OCEAN
WE ALL SHARE TOGETHER

MY FAVORITE SELF HELP BOOKS AND INSPIRATIONAL BOOKS IN NO PARTICULAR ORDER

- ⬦ *A NEW EARTH* BY ECKHART TOLLE
- ⬦ *THE POWER OF NOW* BY ECKHART TOLLE
- ⬦ *CATCHING THE BIG FISH* BY DAVID LYNCH
- ⬦ *THE BIG LEAP* BY GAY HENDRICKS
- ⬦ *UNBOUND: A WOMAN'S GUIDE TO POWER* BY KAJIA URBANIAK

- ⬦ *THE VEIN OF GOLD* BY JULIA CAMERON
- ⬦ *LOVING WHAT IS* BY BYRON KATIE
- ⬦ *EMERGENT STRATEGY* BY adrienne maree brown
- ⬦ *HOW TO DO NOTHING* BY JENNY ODELL
- ⬦ *COMPLEX PTSD: FROM SURVIVING TO THRIVING* BY PETE WALKER

ACKNOWLEDGEMENTS

THANK YOU TO MY AGENT LAURIE ABKEMEIER FOR EVERYTHING—AND FOR GIVING NEW LIFE TO THIS BOOK.

THANK YOU TO MY EDITOR KATIE GOULD FOR YOUR *INFINITE* PATIENCE.

THANK YOU TO ALL MY READERS, FANS, AND CHAMPIONS WHO HAVE SUPPORTED MY WORK OVER THE YEARS, WITH AN EXTRA SPECIAL THANK YOU TO SKYLIGHT BOOKS FOR SUPPORTING THE EARLY ZINE INCARNATION OF THIS BOOK.

THANK YOU TO RAINA LEE, JADE CHANG, AND KRYSTAL CHANG FOR OUR TIME TOGETHER AT SALMON CREEK FARM. THANK YOU TO FRITZ LAEG FOR MAKING SCF AND ALL ITS MAGIC ACCESSIBLE TO US.

THANK YOU TO MY FRIENDS AND FAMILY. I LOVE YOU ALL SO, SO MUCH.

THANK YOU TO ALL THE COUNTLESS TEACHERS, ARTISTS, VISIONARIES, HEALERS — KNOWN AND UNKNOWN — WHO HAVE ALL COME BEFORE ME.

THANK YOU GEORGE FOR THE ENDLESS HUGS AND SUPPORT. ♡

THANK YOU STEPHANIE KNOX STEINER FOR INTRODUCING ME TO ECKHART TOLLE!

ABOUT THE AUTHOR

YUMI SAKUGAWA IS A SECOND-GENERATION JAPANESE-OKINAWAN AMERICAN INTERDISCIPLINARY ARTIST BASED IN LOS ANGELES AND THE AUTHOR OF SEVERAL BOOKS, INCLUDING *I THINK I AM IN FRIEND-LOVE WITH YOU* AND *YOUR ILLUSTRATED GUIDE TO BECOMING ONE WITH THE UNIVERSE.* @YUMISAKUGAWA